FOREST BOOKS

STOLEN FIRE

LYUBOMIR LEVCHEV was born on 29 April 1935, in the town of Troyan in the foothills of the Balkan range in central Bulgaria. He attended secondary school in Sofia, graduating from Kliment Ochrid University, Sofia in the faculties of Philosophy and History. In his career he has been an editor of a daily newspaper, a radio programme organizer, an editor of the weekly newspaper of the Writers' Union, Literary Front, first vice-president of the Committee for Culture, and first Deputy Minister for Culture. At present he is President of the Bulgarian Writers' Union. He has received several major literary prizes including the French Academy's Gold Medal and title of Chevalier de l'Ordre de la Poésie in 1985.

EWALD OSERS was born in Prague in 1917 but has lived in the United Kingdom since 1938. A writer and lecturer, he has translated over eighty books, twenty one of them poetry volumes. A fellow of the Royal Society of Literature, he has been awarded many prizes and in 1983 was given the Silver Pegasus of the Bulgarian Writers' Union.

JACQUELINE CROFTON was born in London in 1946. From the age of 13 she studied at Harrow School of Art and has since developed her own distinctive style. Her particular interest is non-sycophantic portraiture especially in the medium of charcoal. She has exhibited at many exhibitions and her work has been printed by silk screen in limited editions.

STOLEN
FIRE

SELECTED POEMS
by
LYUBOMIR LEVCHEV

translated from the Bulgarian
by
EWALD OSERS
with a foreword
by
JOHN BALABAN
and illustrations
by
JACQUELINE CROFTON

FOREST BOOKS/UNESCO

LONDON ☆ 1986 ☆ BOSTON

UNESCO Collection of Representative Works
European Series

This book has been accepted in the translations
collection of the United Nations Educational Scientific
and Cultural Organisation (UNESCO)

Published by FOREST BOOKS
20 Forest View, Chingford, London E4 7AY, U.K.
61 Lincoln Road, Wayland, M.A. 01788, U.S.A.

First published 1986

Typeset in Great Britain by Cover to Cover, Cambridge
Printed in Great Britain by A. Wheaton & Co Ltd, Exeter

Jacket design © Dixie
Illustrations © Jacqueline Crofton
Original work: © Lyubomir Levchev c/o JUSAUTOR, Sofia 1986
English translation and introduction © UNESCO, 1986
Translated from the Bulgarian and introduction by Ewald Osers

British Library Cataloguing in Publication Data
Levchev, Lyubomir
Stolen Fire: selected poems:
I. Title   II. Osers, Ewald
891'.8'113   PG1037.L4/
ISBN 0–948259–04–3

Library of Congress Catalog Card Number
85–082112

Acknowledgements

Poems have been taken from the following volumes:

Salute to the Fire (1978)
Afterlove (1980)
Fragment (1980)
Incantations (1981)

Contents

Foreword

A few years ago, while in Bulgaria on a translation project, I spent an interesting twenty-four hours with Lyubomir Levchev. Some account of that visit may give the reader another sense of the complex man who is the author of these poems, for besides his being a celebrated poet, Mr. Levchev is also the President of the Union of Bulgarian Writers and a member of the Central Committee of the Communist party which runs the affairs of his country. As President of the Writers Union, he guides not only the careers of individual writers, but also the literary interests of Bulgaria, including making Bulgarian literature known throughout the world. Now, how could *a poet* accomplish this diversity of tasks? One would expect a cold bureaucrat with a highly interior private self (where poems are sequestered). Instead, one finds Levchev open, robust, generous, and thoroughly engaged in whatever momentary drama he is in . . . and for him these are many and diverse.

As I said, I had been busy at translations for about three weeks one December, settled in at the deserted Writers Villa on the Black Sea. On my return to Sofia, Levchev offered me a diversion: boar hunting in the Pirin mountains near the Greek border. We left on Saturday before dawn. I remember Levchev's loaning me a pair of his boots, some heavy wool socks, a sheepskin overcoat, and a wonderful sheathknife from his collection. At Bansko, around 8:30 that morning, our small party of writers met up with some local province officials. The snow was already deep in the town. We parked Levchev's Mercedes and drove in a jeep up logging trails into the steep, snow-bound mountains where the wind was raking the crusted hemlocks. At around 8,000 feet, we met up with another twenty or so men, huddled about a huge fire burning on the snow: roughcut men who clearly knew the mountains as home. They did not know I was coming but seemed amused to have an American in tow. Nor did they seem overawed to have a Central Committee member with them. Levchev, for all his obvious importance in

Bulgaria, has an easy and familiar way, a genuine example, I thought, of the kind of down-home manner which American politicians like to cultivate.

We hunted all day, hidden behind hemlocks as the drivers hooted towards us in numbing cold. None of the writers even had a shot, but the local man dragged in two huge boars when we gathered again at the bonfire of railway ties at the end of the day, eating sausages and drinking slibova until our cold toes tingled and heads swam with the alcohol and brisk air. I thought that was it. Exhausted, I was looking forward to the warm ride home.

But Levchev had other plans. He likes to let things unfold. We drove out of the mountains to Sandanski where the poet, Peter Karaagnov, was being given a large public celebration on his 50th birthday. The municipal hall was jammed with local television and radio crews, with your Pioneers in uniforms and red scarves, with Peter's editorial colleagues, with army representatives, with Party officials and with a crowd of well-wishers. Levchev, then nearly 50 himself, was remarkably unexhausted from his day, and somehow now in a suit and tie as the master of ceremonies at the podium, fresh as a Spring Beauty, while I sat, wilted, among the guests of honor on the stage. The thing went on for two hours. Levchev seemed to know everyone and called forth, in turn, laughter and sentimental silence from the audience. Under the spotlights, hot, hungover and hungry, I wondered how he could hold up so well, so long. I realized gradually that he was having a great time of it.

Then the banquet. A huge hall by an icy river. Guests slow to arrive. Levchev again presiding, greeting guests, offering toasts around the long tables, saluting Peter Karaagnov who was looking both proud and embarrased. It was 10:00 PM. After more drinks and before any dinner, I slunk out to sleep on the backseat of the Mercedes. Later, I remember being shaken awake by the driver and seeing behind him an animated and annoyed Levchev. They had been looking for me everywhere. 'John,' he was saying, I think in English, 'you blew it. Now you'll miss Vanga.' Vanga is an extraordinary blind woman who has a long reputation as a clairvoyant. I had expressed interest in meeting her some weeks before. Levchev, who likes to make things happen, had remembered, and while not telling me, had made her a part of our agenda too. So, after some driving around on dark snowy roads, we found her around midnight as our car crossed a small wooden bridge and met the car she was riding in. She is frail and beginning to age. She was on her way to the hospital because her heart was fluttering. Levchev was positively sweet and deferential with her. He apologized for bothering her, and called me over to her car, putting my hands in her hands as he introduced me. This was not the public voice of the master of ceremonies, but gentler and full of solicitude. Vanga held my hand for a moment and then touched my face. She told Levchev that I was 'a nice young man,' and he smiled his boyish grin and nodded and we both thanked her and said goodbye.

I slept most of the way back to Sofia, my hair matted from my hunting cap and the exertions of the day and evening, my face still wind-burned from the gusts howling through the Pirin. I leaned against the window or against the madcap poet Bozhidar Bozhilov, snoring beside me. From time to time, I heard Levchev talking with the other writers and then, when they nodded off to sleep one by one, to his driver. Levchev has an easy way of talking, interrupted by bursts of humor. It is the relaxed talk of a man fully confident of himself and liking the world around him. There's something enormously healthy about him.

John Balaban
The Pennsylvania State University

Introduction

The fact that the poetry of Eastern and South-eastern Europe is still largely unknown to English and American readers is due to a number of reasons. One of them, of course, is the relative inaccessibility and supposed difficulty of the languages of t⊦ region – 'languages of limited diffusion' in Unesco's official terminology – but another is a certain cultural insularity, and at times hubris, on the part of our literary Establishment. That Russia, a great empire, could have an important literature was eventually conceded about the turn of the century, largely thanks to such translators as Constance Garnett; but the suggestion that small nations like the Czechs, Slovaks, Hungarians, Serbs, Romanians, Bulgarians or Albanians could have great poets was until not so long ago viewed with profound mistrust and scepticism. Even the modern Greeks, in spite of the persisting foothold of a classical education among the British Establishment right up to the Second World War, tended to be disregarded as a nation where 'all except their sun has set'. It was probably due to George Seferis, the poet and (luckily for modern Greek poetry) diplomat posted to London, that British poetry lovers suddenly awoke to one of the many strands of contemporary Balkan poetry.

The late fifties and early sixties witnessed a sudden emergence of interest in poetry abroad. *Modern Poetry in Translation* edited by Daniel Weissbort – while not the first periodical devoted exclusively to translated poetry (I remember Neville Braybrooke's *Translation* at the end of the war) – was a pioneer in the field. An enormous impact was also made by Penguin's *Modern European Poets* series (with A. Alvarez as the series editor). There were (and, unlike Penguin and Cape, still are) the smaller poetry publishers Carcanet, Anvil, Menard, and more recently Bloodaxe and Forest Books. Few of the other publishers showed the same enduring commitment to modern translated poetry as the ones I have named.

Not all literatures have been equally well served. Languages with substantial diffusion, due to pre-war or immediate post-war emigration of their native speakers to Britain, have done best: German, Czech, Polish and Greek (mainly from Cyprus). Romanian poetry appeared on the English scene a little later, Bulgarian poetry (in book form) is appearing here for the first time, and Macedonian and Albanian poetry (I happen to know that some interesting work is being written in both these languages) has not so far been published in the U.K. at all.

Most English readers will be surprised to learn that Bulgarian literature has in fact a long, though not (in written form) continuous, tradition. The earliest extant texts in Old Slavonic date from the late ninth century; a real flowering of Bulgarian writing (both ecclesiastical and secular-folkloristic) occurred towards the end of the fourteenth century. During the centuries of Turkish occupation of the Balkans, including the territory of Bulgaria, the language survived but, in the absence of a normative written literary language, existed in a number of dialectal forms. It was not until the nineteenth century that, along with parallel movements in other minority, or pariah languages of Central and Eastern Europe, the intellectuals of the National Revival strove to create, or recreate, a literary form of Bulgarian. And, again as elsewhere among unfree nations of Europe, this revivalist enthusiam seemed to release a wealth of pent-up creative energy: Bulgarian poetry, at first looking to Russian and German literary models, soon produced a fine flowering.

After the Second World War the most important milestone in Bulgarian poetry – as indeed also in Polish, Czech, Hungarian and, for a while, Soviet poetry – was the onset of de-Stalinization, associated in Bulgaria with the overthrow of Chervenkov in 1956. This cultural liberalization is known in Bulgarian poetry as the 'April line'. It does not, in my opinion, represent (as some would claim) the victory of the 'modernists' over the 'traditionalists'. It does mean – and this is probably a much healthier state of affairs – that 'modernism', or any other

-ism, is now not only permitted but entirely respectable. Looking at Bulgarian literary journals one gets the impression that the two great streams, 'modernism' and 'traditionalism', continue to coexist. Nor would it be correct to assume that the younger generation of poets are all 'modernists'; some of them are decidedly traditional, and others seem to have a foot in both camps.

There can be no doubt where Lyubomir Levchev stands. He is a 'modernist' and indeed is regarded by many as their standard-bearer. Born in 1935, he published his first book of poetry in 1957. Its very title *The Stars Belong to Me* seemed provocative. A German critic (Wolf Oschlies in *Deutsche Studien* 1975), describing the bewilderment the volume caused among Bulgarian critics, who were unsure of the reaction expected from them, suggested that it had been lucky for them that 'Bulgarian has but one word (*dărzost*) for "boldness" and "impertinence".' For twenty years critics in Bulgaria and the West have been calling his poetry 'controversial'.

Levchev was not the 'angry young man' some Western critics made him out to be: he was far too happy, too full of vitality, too prone to disrespectful laughter for that role. He was a gifted extrovert, even at times an exhibitionist, an unruly, self-willed individualist who, nevertheless, in an undogmatic way, believed in the political system under which he lived. But he refused to toe any political or literary line:

> *Listen,*
> *You*
> *who keep extending your hands:*
> *My soul is made*
> *of rebellious matter!*
> *Did you hear –*
> > *matter!*
> *You heard correctly –*
> > *rebellious!*

And in response to calls that he should at long last 'take up a position' he replied contemptuously:

> *Only the dead*
> *maintain their position . . .*

To appreciate how shocking Levchev seemed, one must remember that Bulgarian poetry had been less influenced by literary trends from abroad than that of Czechoslovakia, Hungary, Greece, and even Romania; Mayakovskiy's influence had been a passing one in the twenties. Most Bulgarian poetry up to the mid-century had been entirely traditionalist.

In an interesting interview given to the West German *Volkszeitung* in 1979 Levchev described Blok, Yesenin and Mayakovskiy as his 'teachers'; Akhmadullina, Voznesenskiy and Yevtushenko had been his 'class-mates'. After listing Lorca, Machado, Alberti, Neruda and Guillen as formative influences, he went on: 'I have also learned a very great deal from T. S. Eliot. Especially craftsmanship. I am often asked: How is it that the poet and communist Levchev has anything to learn from a Catholic reactionary like Eliot? What I learned from him was neither Catholicism nor reaction, but how to write verse. I learned from him that verses can be written not only the way one speaks but also the way one thinks.'

I would say that he learned something else from T. S. Eliot: the easy, almost imperceptible, switch between formal (at times almost hieratic) language and a conversational tone: 'an easy commerce of the old and the new, the common word exact without vulgarity, the formal word precise but not pedantic'. Like no other contemporary Bulgarian poet he lives – demonstratively, provocatively – in two worlds which the cultural hard-liners would regard as incompatible: the world of political and civic commitment, and a private sensual world. In a 'confessional' poem (*The Law*) he observes that 'the kings of the snobbish cafés' – we in the West would call them the literary Popes – will never forgive him for singing of the smoke of the Kremikovtsi steelworks, Bulgaria's national symbol of modernization, and at the same time enjoying Gershwin's music and Eliot's poetry. And if he were not such a good and original poet he probably would not have got away with it at the time before he became a national figure. It may well be that future literary critics will regard this break-away from the traditional concepts of what, and how, a socialist poet should write, this unshackling of contemporary poetry, as his most important contribution.

Over the years Levchev's provocative irreverance

diminished, and private themes began to take up more room in his poetry. Since 1957 he has occupied various positions in literary journalism and in the official hierarchy, being editor-in-chief of the weekly newspaper *Literaturen Front* and, since 1976, a full member of the Communist Party's Central Committee. He is now President of the Union of Bulgarian Writers. He has received several major literary prizes – including the French Academy's Gold Medal and title *Chevalier de l'Ordre de la Poésie* in 1985 – and his poetry is increasingly appearing abroad. Indeed, volumes of Levchev's poetry have now been published in twenty-one countries. Forest Books deserves the gratitude of all poetry lovers for raising this total to twenty-two by bringing out the first Levchev volume in the United Kingdom.

Ewald Osers

CONFESSION AND
SALUTE TO THE FIRE

Interrogated by
whips of my own imperfection
I've no strength left . . .
I confess . . .

I confess that
poetry is a criminal attempt
to translate
the pulsations of the universe
into the simple mortal language of our hearts.

I confess:
poetry is brazen witchcraft.
Poetry permits
the gods
to assume
human shape
and simultaneously brands humans with divinity.

I confess
that from the very beginning I was aware
that such witchcraft was punishable
by burning at the stake.

And so –
hail, our poetic
life-giving, death-bringing Fire!
Brothers and sisters at the stake,
I pay homage to your ashes.
And totally surrender myself to you,
my red,
my warlike love!

DIMINUTIVES

A road
and childhood memories surrounding it.
(Unexpectedly I'm passing through my native region again.)
Long white clouds
under a tapestry sky.
Thin and rhythmical clouds
above me
above everything . . .

I'm intoxicated by the perfume
of your deception,
my love.
Please
don't kiss me at the bends.
Nor when I'm blinded by the headlights of oncoming vehicles
either.

White clouds
and an indigo universe.
White
as a skeleton.
And between the ribs of Death
throb billions of dear little stars . . .

Mother, mother!
How I hate these diminutives.
And how you love them!

Me
and those diminutives,
how you love us!
– Is your dear little shirt clean? –
you'll be asking me
if I get back in time.

But why am I not loved
by dear little time,
mother?
Maybe
because I overtake it.

Maybe
because I finish its work for it . . .
because I command it . . .

I know that in the end time will have its revenge.
Today it pretends to be dead
but tomorrow it will dance on my dead body
a dear little country dance . . .

Except that till tomorrow there's so much time!

A road
and childhood memories surrounding it . . .

PRAYER FOR
A BEGINNING AND AN END

In order to live
according to the laws of beauty
one must believe.
One must believe!

> That's how
> your prayer begins,
> atheist!

Believe
in the divinity of the burning fire
if you have tamed the domestic hearth!
If not,
then
believe
in the wild hunted flame!
Go insane!
Kiss
the banner of love!
And whisper sacred curses
till your lips crack,
till instead of words
blood spurts
and mingles with the fire . . .
and the wing of pain carries you up . . .

Believe
always with open eyes!
Believe in the improbable!
Believe in comradeship . . .
whenever you attack . . .
And whenever the traitor's
elegant bullets hit you
repeat:
– In order to live
according to the laws of beauty
one must believe!

6

I now think,
clinging
to the edge of my precipitous experience:
The easiest thing
and the pleasantest is
to believe in lies.

– Hey, organizer
of collective miracles,
if you find you're continually happy
better check out your beliefs!

The most difficult thing
and the greatest is
to believe
in merciless truth.

There,
you're going,
you, twentieth century, are running out . . .
xx
Even the Roman numeral
reminds you of clenched teeth.
You're marching and stumbling
over the corpses of half-dead deities.

The air is polluted
with the smell of rotting religions.
The aircraft –
our last angels –
drink up the oxygen.
And the sky rumbles angrily.
You're weary
and convinced
all that knowledge is unbearable:
Dates.
Distances.
Addresses.
Titles.
Quotations.
Secrets . . .

Ah, well,
but when eventually you feel
that time
no longer flows
through you?

You want to die beautifully

Everyone wants to die beautifully.

Not till then
do you realize
that you lack sufficient information
for that last,
most important task . . .

And you repeat:
One must believe!

                    That's how
                    your prayer ends,
                    atheist!

In order to die beautifully
one must believe!
One must believe devoutly.
One must believe ardently!
One must believe . . .
Even more!

THAT FEELING FOR HISTORY

The signal on the track dawns reseda-coloured.
The window for farewells is open . . .

Only immortals possess
that feeling for history.

A feeling?

And we mortals?
We say goodbye
with a kiss on the old-fashioned platform . . .

And yet I know,
I know
one immortal –
the most immortal of all –
the people!

Like every man in love
you jump on a moving train,
push
into that cheerful
and dreary
hard-seat class.
You feel knees and elbows.
You feel that eager current
flowing right through you.
And this night train passes –
a marvellous punctuation of winking lights
that feeling for history.

History!
And so the two of you travel.
And so you travel
through yourself
and through the universe.
Then suddenly you emerge from your tunnels
and cross the enchanted bridge
called 'Today' . . .

Yet beneath you gleams Lethe . . .

O traveller,
if you feel
that the feeling for history
no longer flows through you
it means you've lost
your link with the Immortal.

It means you've alighted at some wayside stop
for a quick wash
under the rusty pump . . .
And
suddenly the train's gone.
And you're alone.
Only a light like some receding star
is vanishing towards distant crucifixions . . .

No!
I've not missed my time!
Nor will my time miss me.
I hear the pounding of hearts
testing the track,
secret tunnels piercing the rock,
passages to something inaccessible.
I'm travelling on this overcrowded train,
breathing the defiance
of these tired workers
and through me, elating me, flows
again
intoxicating me,
that feeling for history.

THE FORTRESS

We're standing on Tsar Samuel's fortress!
Before us
Belasitsa Mountain –
a symbol of destiny.
And then
the running streams – a brown unfinished epic.
A ringing of two-edged flashes of sunlight . . .
The Bulgarian sky here leans
on Tumba, Konguro and Kalabak . . .

We're standing on Tsar Samuel's fortress!

And now I hear
and now I feel
a deep black subterranean voice:
– Hey, One-Eyed One,
tell us what you can see
from Samuel's unceasing worry.

I reply:
I can see people
sowing,
and I can see people growing like their corn.
I can see people who have faith
and who are setting out
on a frightening road . . .
And I can also see the Bulgar-killers.
And the traitors, fanning
their paid-for little fire . . .

. . .   But you, my distant forebear,
my disturbed subterranean ancestor,
don't tremble so the earth quakes.

Who could succeed today in gouging out
the stars of our flags, of our hearts,
of our dedication?
This is not the year
ten fourteen!

Now on the road – alive and not sung to the end
I can see
teachers are teaching creation,
builders are building a world of dreams,
dreamers are trying to sing the road to its end . . .

And so
the wheel of the universe turns
between light and darkness.

. . . But in our hearts
Belasitsa Mountain
is a symbol of destiny.
The unfinished epic courses in our blood.
And flashes of sunlight our baptism . . .

The Bulgarian sky here leans
on Tumba, Konguro and Kalabak . . .

And something else
I see –
all of us once more
are standing on Tsar Samuel's fortress!

                        Petrich, April 1978

(Note: On 29 July 1014 the Bulgarian armies here engaged in battle with Basil II
'Bulgaroktonos' – the Bulgar-killer – and were destroyed. All men who were not
killed were blinded; only one, their leader, was allowed to keep one eye.
Samuel's fortress now is just a green hill on the bank of the Strumeshnitsa, near
the town of Petrich. The peaks Tumba, Konguro and Kalabak frame the high
ridge of Belasitsa Mountain.)

THE ROAD FROM THE ORIENT
AND THE ROAD TO THE ORIENT

I'm a worker.
I'm tired.
I'm returning alone
on the autobahn
half asleep . . .

I work in a very alien country.
I work in a factory below ground.
And don't even know what I am producing.
Strictly secret!
Perhaps there I've been producing
the very secrets of the universe . . .
Forgive me . . .
forgive me – I don't know.

But every evening
I climb into my dream
and return.

I'm driving nervously.
I'm driving fast
because
my home is a long, long way away.
Before me yawns a second infinity.
E5 – the 'Road of death'.
And my girl
writes she can't wait for me any longer . . .

Yes,
Tonight I'm driving very nervously.
Yes, memories and crossroads,
I jump the red light . . .
But stop your condescending
sighs
and plastic grimaces!
Dear spectators,
all I want is to get home!

Nothing else!

(Do you know how cruel it is
to be poor in such a rich country
which can afford to import even
poor wretches from the Orient . . .)

That moment everything is illuminated
by the falling moon.
It pounces
almost in front of me,
blending with the driving wheel . . .
As if I were steering the sky . . .

Stop!
I've got to start again at the beginning.
Because I do not seek to steer anyone
and don't want anyone to steer me!
I've got to start again at the beginning:

I'm a worker.
I'm tired.
I'm returning dead-alone
on the autobahn
half asleep . . .
I'm returning to my Orient.

What have you infected me with, you –
saviours,
employers, robots?
I don't understand the hills.
I don't recognize the trees.
I've forgotten the language of rivers . . .
Now
I only know the road
and only the road knows me –
the road from the Orient
and the road to the Orient.

That's spooled up in me like a ciné-film,
coiled like the spring of a clock.
Like a snake,
venomous and
sacred . . .

And you can't miss the road.
On both sides
instead of milestones
are rusting skeletons of dreams
and blind birds land on crumpled wings of cars . . .

Sometimes I stop.
To let the engine rest.
It's cooling now
and something's muttering.
Its radiator ribs vibrate.
And I'm lying
on some enormous drum
of telephone cable.

I breathe the dirty wind
and my canopy is the merciful stars.
How beautiful it is!
Across the road
a light gleams yellow:
a petrol station,
an altar of the devil.
And inside some young girl dreams
like a fly trapped in amber.
And in the lay-by:
spectres,
fabulous monsters,
TIR trucks.
And in their cabs, redolent with fuel,
my doubles are sleeping,
dreaming of homecomings,
dreaming of love . . .
and that's enough for them.
I ought to wake them –
shout at them:
– Stop fooling yourselves!
Don't fool yourselves as I did!
Dream of struggle,
dream of bullets,
dream implacable
words . . .
I ought to shout to them.

But I've no time,
                    I've no time,
                    I've got to get on . . .
The road I see
starts out from night
and arrives in the night . . .

I suppose you think I'm talking so I won't fall asleep.
I'm simply afraid.
Afraid that these words will choke me.
All these
small,
black,
persistent words.
I feel like a boiled sweet spat out on the road
on which ants are eagerly feasting.

A million years ago
my mother used to say:
– My boy,
everything will pass
as soon as you confess! . . .
I'd agree with her now.
But who to?
If there were one god and one only
I'd give him a lift in my car.
God?
Why is there such a word
When there's no such thing?

All you silent ones –
lightning,
women,
moons,
and darkness,
darkness . . .
All of you used to be –
and maybe will be again –
deities.
But now –
in this present century,
at this opaque moment,
why is there such a word?

17

My dearest,
you were enough
religion for me.
Whenever you drank from my glass
the remaining wine became
heavenly.
And whenever I drank
from your fateful lips
the last drops . . .

But was anything left?

What a magnificent god I'd have in
the girl I love!

Why did she write
she couldn't wait for me any longer?
The law
of every god is
that he waits without end . . .
But you wrote to me . . .
And I know
what's written there
and what isn't.

I know that I'm alone.
I know I'm returning in vain.
Because . . .
I know the Orient has disappeared.
The Orient no longer exists!
Just as God no longer exists.
Only the word is left –
ransacked,
sweetly untrue . . .

I know that everything starts with the word,
but I can't return in a mere word,
even on the autobahn
half asleep.

It's true:
like an idiot
I've turned my life into a motorcar.

For what?
So that I can return to the Orient.
So that some day I can open a door,
loving and laughing.
So I can call out to you:
– Come into my life!
We'll decorate the car
with flowers
and ribbons
and white head scarves,
and drive all our lives as newly-weds!

Now
my life's racing on senselessly
on the autobahn
in a half-dream.
Brilliantly outmoded
and spent.
Bought second-hand
and paid for mercilessly . . .
Now
my life is racing to the Orient.

How shall I begin at the beginning?
Do I deserve to begin at the beginning . . .
From the word . . .
From the sacred words:
I'm a worker!
I . . .

. . . I let go of the wheel,
I press my foot down hard.

And my life races crazily
down the road
to the Orient.
A bright light on the horizon
marks the 24-hour restaurant.

A little later
the axle slips its bearing.

With a leap I leave the asphalt.
A sweet shudder down my spine.
For a second I am flying.
And crash into hardened night.

A metallic pyre flares up.
My wild dream's on fire
off the road.
And my blood's on fire.
And my eyes too.
And the universe is free of charge.

– Expatriate plates.
A trivial incident . . .
The road patrolman writes.
Only a shuttered hut with a barking dog
shows any sympathy.
And the few gapers disperse again.
Drive on!
They climb into their cars again.
One sleepy child
is saying:
– Daddy, look,
falling stars!

Yes, I am leaping across the firmament.
I'm pulling off some nameless stars.
I'll send them to you for remembrance
in August,
my love . . .

Charred.
Instructive.
Gentle.
Charred, unexpected, faithful.
I'm a worker.
I'm off to the building site.
The building site
of matter.

WORDS THAT SLIP OUT

Spring snow
lies on the grass,
wet
and trampled.
A dog –
a mongrel
like me –
sniffs it with cheerful amazement.

Spring snow
lies on the ground,
rather like those old-fashioned
blankets,
knitted
by mother in her youth . . .
The earth smells
of my childhood . . .
           There,
           in the bay at sunset,
           an unemployed worker
           is playing a stringless guitar . . .
I'm listening to him.

Spring life –
I think to myself –
means
mother
has finally managed
to cover everything
with lace covers . . .
How wonderful it all is!
How quickly it melts!

Spring snow
lies –
sugar icing
on a funeral cake . . .

An importunate image!
It begins to irritate me.
As if . . .

Spring snow
lies on my soul
like foam
on the back of a dead-tired foal . . .
Did I say tired?
Nonsense!
That's a word
that slipped out quite, quite accidentally.

A CURSE ON COLUMBUS

Don Cristobal Colòn
or Columbus,
or whatever you like to call yourself –
unlucky man,
naive and
witless.
There is no mercy for you anymore!

You transformed our vision of the world.
You transformed the world itself.
History at once began to be the 'New Age' . . .
There is no pardon for you any more!

Why didn't you listen
to the admiral on the golden mainland
when he urged you in a whisper:
– Listen,
my dear fellow,
listen!
You absorb storms
and unprecedented spaces,
but don't ever forget me!
Because
the most important thing ultimately
is me,
with whom you took tea!

And thus
the noblemen of Spain
are bored.
It is said,
Columbus,
that you're a crook.
You sail off to the West for the sheer joy of it . . .
And the route you've discovered
is not to India at all,
the devil knows where it's to . . .
And besides –

instead of praying
you get drunk
and go whoring . . .
Curse you!
Curse you!!
Curse you!!!

Surely you understand
what lies ahead of you?

Your continent will bear a stranger's name.
And as for you –
whip and derision,
syphilis and ruin!

Don Cristobal Colòn,
why aren't you miserable?
Why don't you crawl on your knees?
Why are you hanging about
the waterside contentedly
with the leprous beggars?
You're searching for something.
A cloud?
Or a ghost?
A medusa among the stars?

You really are a revolting man!
You're a monster!
You can see something after all!
You can see . . .
something we still cannot discern ourselves .

Genoa, 1977

24

HOLY VICTORY

Not of my own volition
is something choosing me . . .

I've always been a friend of loners,
of the doomed, the condemned, etc.
Cognac and beer
in that little restaurant at the station . . .
No sooner had they succeeded
than they forgot me . . .
And I them, of course . . .

Only you, Cézanne, are stubborn still.
You are a bad character, Paul.
(What can I do?)

There you sit, drawing,
drawing,
to the last ray of light.
Victoire.
Sainte Victoire!
Holy Victory!

That mountain –
why is it
always before your eyes?
Why does it walk before you?
In the end won't it move aside
to give way to a new picture,
or, just
so one can see
if there is anything behind it?

Maybe a road will speak out.
Maybe a sacred river will see.
Victoire,
Sainte Victoire!
Holy Victory!

And in the end they will all shout
that you're a genius,
that all threads start from you . . .

But this no longer satisfies anything.
Fame is not a good companion.
From this point onward words are mere confusion . . .
Victoire,
Sainte Victoire!
Holy Victory!

Paris, 1978

(Note: St. Victoire, a mountain in Provence, was the almost obsessive motif of Cézanne during the final 10 years of his life. An exhibition of his paintings of that period was held in Paris in 1978.)

OUR NATIVE LAND
AND THE FREEDOM WITHIN US

Bulgaria,
forgive my
untutored intoxication!
But I'm celebrating,
and everything within me is celebrating,
one century since your rebirth as a nation.
Bulgaria,
your freedom celebrates within me,
the sun's eyes are triumphing,
the wind's hair is dancing.
The ice is melting on the giant peaks
tumultuously,
those of Etropol and Troyan.
And my romantic voice rings out in ardour,
leaping the breakwater
in Burgas harbour.
The cockerels of Blagoevgrad awake within me –
those faithful trumpeters –
heralding the day.
I hear them clearly:
I've flung wide open the shutters of
my crazy little room in this hotel,
'The Crimson Poppy'.
But I couldn't sleep
in this hotel bed: far too deep
went the excitement of the celebration
at my Maritsa Mouth, my Devni, my Kremikovtsi . . .
And on they sail,
they sail,
they sail,
those Danube swans,
those improbable swans, on those furious whirlpools . . .

Bulgaria,
native land, permit me
this love-choked explanation,
now
that your name has a new solemn ring
and this is the centenary of your liberation . . .

Let me salute the blood that bought your miracle.
The freedom, and that proud and wild belief
that a heroic death alone revives . . .
To that proud madness I now pledge my life.

After five centuries of sacrifice,
Bulgaria,
at the supreme hour,
selfless as nature,
with elemental power,
great Russia died for you.
And many other holy mothers
have died through you
for freedom.
They died, exalted
as your saviours,
for what they did not have themselves.

Now
I feel
our fruitful black-earth throbs
with living
and long-vanished people.
The International of the blood
pulses deep down,
producing sap
and strength
for the feelings which have raised us high.

I'm proud that your freedom is
the sister of freedom everywhere,
Bulgaria.
And therefore
find it easy to discern
even wordlessly,
who your comrades are.

Bulgaria,
tradition handed down
for perpetuity,
for every sacred goal . . .

Bulgaria –
like life,
no,
like the mystery of life itself . . .
Bulgaria –
and only from heart
to heart.

Bulgaria,
my April faith,
unfold and burn,
so that I may take fire!

Bulgaria,
love
and curse
and ordained fate,
Bulgaria,
with you to the end,
through you and for you may I stand!

A FLASH OF SOLITUDE

I'm not a recluse.
I'm only a lone wolf.
I'm – a person who likes others . . .
I eat biscuits
and revolting sandwiches
scattered all over the countryside
by inconsiderate tourists.
An empty tin gleams full of rain.
I could read the newspaper here,
but I don't feel like it –
I'll become a dog . . .
God, this forest's boring!
Today
I came across a huntsman.
He took aim at me through his telescopic sight
but didn't fire.
He shook with fright
in case he killed me . . .
Because I'm under the protection of the law.

WORKERS' BLOOD

The collar of my soul is blue.
The blood with which I write
is red.

I shall pass
through this exploding universe
like insane love
like righteous anger.

Day alone has a right to night!
Work alone has a right to a break!
Here am I uttering these thunderous phrases.
Good
or bad,
that's how you made me,
you –
my
inherited
worker's blood.

I'd like to be a builder –
throwing epic bridges
over suffered
disappointments . . .
or building a new world . . .

I'd like to be a steelworker –
breathing hardness into alloys
and hardness into people.
I'd like . . .

But my blood now
commands me
to do battle.

But what kind of battle?
Without barricades!
Be hard-working.
Be dapper.
Be an official.

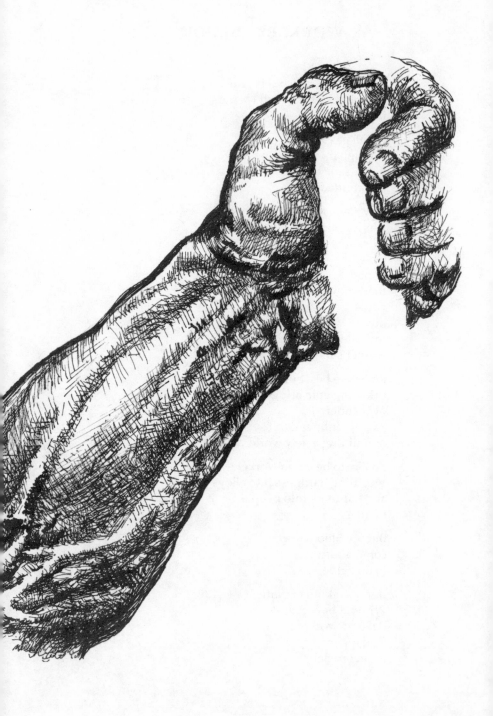

And plunge into hell.
And then . . .
remain
ardent and pure.
Write with your blood.
Be a ballad.
Be a poet – a communist . . .

Communists at the close of the twentieth century,
our task today is certainly no easier!
Communists in jail,
Communists in power –
on each of us the same sentence is passed!

Again they're setting us against each other.
With brown and yellow venom they're poisoning us:
'Don't attack them!
Don't anger them!
Leave them to their own dissensions!'
And the extremes embrace each other
and into this enchanted circle
the faithless bullet strikes
and then
you flow –
worker's blood . . .

Now you are life's haemoglobin.
You are the ink of universal history.
You speak within me
in the language of the stolen fire.

You're the whiplash of the great alarm.
And if I dream of cosmic risings,
and if in my ventures
I try to be first,
I owe it all to you –
my art,
my inheritance,
my bequest –
my worker's blood!

THE LOCAL DANCE

Dance –
magician
hidden in the very depth of me.
Dance in everyone of us . . .

        Trance.
        Touching
        the full moon with a crown of thorns.
        A prehistoric and delightful demon!

I
watch the flames from bodies
coming to life,
exploding
the Sunday wasteland.
I burn
and turn
to you: Dance,
you return
us to our beginnings!
(Try to return
to where no one can
return –
Oh, isn't
this
art
and redemption –
dance?)
While they dance,
chance
girls unwittingly reveal to you their secrets.

And you, unwittingly, respond
like a guitar left outside in the wind . . .

I burn
and turn
to you: Dance
you release me from the prison
of chilly thoughts,
revealing to me
the rhythm's legacy,

revealing to me
the birth of dance.
Creation . . .
and love . . .
That I may see how the gods dance
and how the victims dance
in dreams about their murderers . . .

I bow to you
our sad
and cheerful
and ceaseless madness –
dance!

And maybe everything upon this earth
dances its own magnificent dance!
Here
aerials
twisted by the local wind
are dancing on the roof opposite
a round dance of aluminium skeletons.
Yes,
inhuman skeletons of something
that has long perished in us humans –
and still it feels like dancing . . .

I can hear it . . .

Now
standing at the door
of the club,
I watch the flames of the bodies . . .
I am turning white . . .
But I have not refused a dance.

You're being asked to dance by loneliness,
inwardly I
dance with her.
She presses herself against me
and slowly leads me
to rope bridges,
to sweet oblivion
which
at once
unites me with the entire universe.

THE WORLD OF THE UNKNOWN

'If a man is born to be hanged
he cannot drown.'

Eastern proverb

Before laughing ill-manneredly,
before turning and going away,
let me relate this instructive story,
this intimate parable.

We were living as tenants
in that romantic
magnificent tumble-down building,
the property of death.
A moth – a black one –
had got in.
The rent had just been paid.
And maybe
that's why
my sister,
my dear kid sister,
was studying medicine.
On the table,
laid for a meal,
on top of a textbook
sagely rested a human skull.
On it
I could
show you to this day
(and no worse than the elegant early Valéry)
where the
Sella turcica
is, and where the
Apertura interna
canaliculi nervi petrosi
superficialis minoris.
Words remembered by mere chance,

37

O senseless knowledge
of youthful life without supervision!
To me
that skull served,
just as it had Hristo Botev
(and Nikola Slavkov
and his brother Drasov
when they had their picture taken),
just as
a symbol . . .
It's a symbol of a doom without terror,
It's a symbol of struggle,
of death of immortality . . .
It's an incantation!

More and more so, to me . . .

But then
the anonymous skull
had become very much like a member
of our family.
We weren't afraid of it.
We weren't repelled.
It rested on the table,
elevated
on its pedestal of books,
and haughtily with condescension gazed
upon our sufferings,
upon our agonies and passions . . .

One day . . .
in that room,
where anyone could turn up
and disappear –

        suburban moons . . .
        a barren cherry-tree . . .
        the winds . . .
One day . . .

        I shall never forget this!

One day . . .
entering the room,
before switching on the lamp
I saw
in the skull's
eye-sockets
something glowing.

Mystic occurrences, of course, are not allowed!

It proved to be –
a firefly.
A firefly that had come in through the window of summer,
and then through the window of the room,
and then through the window of the skull,
and then . . .

Then the skull of that unknown person
gently seized me
with its invisible hand.
And led me away . . .

It began by saying:
– I am, you see,
a boy with a hollowed-out melon lantern!
And then I disappeared among the fireflies.
I dissolved in summer's breath.
I lived amidst
the rattle of the ancient stocking factory.
I contemplated
th secrets of the women working there,
the weaving frames,
the silk
and the thread –
gleaming in the labyrinth
of the Minotaur . . .

And afterwards
we stopped outside the gate . . .
under the bright electric bulb . . .
under that chandelier of demented moths . . .

A solitary light,
a solitary feast
in green and infinite fields . . .

And the night-watchman
was standing there with his militia rifle.
– What are you guarding, old man? –
I asked him.
And he answered:
– Here begins the kingdom of the unknown.

And we walked on.
We –

> citizens of eternity
> and subjects of infinity,
> purified,
> unknown,
> unending.

Myself
and the anonymous skull –
hand in hand . . .

And here
begins another song,
which will remain unknown . . .
like the warriors
for whom
the eternal flame dances,
like the girls
for whom
we die partly with our souls
and partly with our bodies . . .

And so –
now –
the time has come for me to laugh,
> to turn
> and go away . . .

I don't expect forgiveness
from anyone
for having ridden the heavenly horses.

But you,
dear friends,
confessors, tale-bearers, slanderers,
in what threats are you trying to entrap me,
in what frightful destruction . . .
in what disastrous flood,
in what cosmic cataclysms?
Don't bother!
It's naive
because I know the road . . .

> The road that leads
> to the kingdom of the unknown!

To where a billion youngsters are on the march
with hollowed-out melon lanterns.

A TASTE FOR THE PRESENT

Wherever I live,
Wherever I die –
in the morning,
early
in the morning
when
stars become people
hurrying anonymously
with the early shift
on powered conveyor belts
to their baptism of fire,
and I amongst them
and on the way chewing
a sandwich
as cold
as the body of God . . .
when it is no longer dark
and not yet light . . .
just at that moment
I experience
an unrepeatable and miraculous
taste for the present.

I'm happy
although I know
how
dangerous it is to be happy.

And my soul is waking happily:
'Hail to thee, dawning and beginning day,
To do my duty I will not delay!'

Wherever I may live,
wherever I may die,
in the evening,

late
in the evening,
when the
people become stars
and return to blue-shirted nebulae,
and I'm amongst them . . .
when it's no longer light
and not yet dark . . .

At just that moment
I
experience
an unforgettable and miraculous
taste for the present.

I'm content
although I know
how
dangerous it is to be content.
And my soul smiles contentedly:
'Farewell, departing and completed day,
To do my duty I will not delay!'

CAPRICE NO. 7

I drank of insincere feelings.
I drank because I was dying of thirst,
    because I was parched,
    because I was already cracking . . .

I drank of insincere feelings –
deceptive,
sticky,
sweet swift-flowing transience!

I drank . .
and now I feel sick.
In the west the sunset is painting
a portrait of my absence.
The bells are ringing.
The Lord is also drinking.
And in my eyes are snow-covered expanses . . .

Oh how I hope my face won't give me away!
I offer my entire kingdom
for just one smile!
Why didn't I die of thirst!

SUPERSTITION

Sharp little beaks are feasting.
And twittering voices triumphant . . .
Sparrows are pecking the old cherry-tree
hanging over
my father's grave.
It doesn't rustle.
Not a leaf stirs.
It knows:
a tree which
curses the birds that rob it
will quickly wither!

I find this green superstition pleasing.
And it hurts me –
but I smile.
This is a distasteful habit!

Am I abnormally conceited
or insensitive?

As if my father had been a stone
and my mother steel.
Besides,
I didn't cry at my father's grave,
although everyone else cried
and wailed
and fainted . . .
And I heard my relations with their hearts of gold
whisper behind my back:
– What an unfeeling child!
– Enfant terrible!

But I don't smile just to infuriate you
or to deprive you of
free entertainment . . .
I'm sorry!
Quite simply, it's the way I'm made –
to breathe happiness,
to have hope jerk from my eyes . . .
And always to proclaim
that green superstition.

Let twittering voices be triumphant then
and sharp little beaks feast on me.

LETTER WRITTEN ON WALLS

To Pierre Seghers

Hello there!
I've received your outcry—
and here I am
hurrying to reply to you . . .

* * *

I can see you returning home –
tired from a complete rest,
eager for insomnia
and inspiration.
A knight –
wounded in so many battles,
mauled by panther,
lion
and starved she-wolf.
I can see you drowning in the Metro –
that dirty underground Louvre –
where disabled and blind men
sing forgettable songs,
where sinners are painting paradise,
where you once painted
'Long live France'
and
'Long live freedom!'
where –
let me admit it –
I once also scribbled
letters of love . . .
I can see you in those endless
passages of underground mankind –
among workmen,
students,
prostitutes,
terrorists,
and tourists . . .

47

I can see you returning home
like a true poet –
from everywhere
to everybody.
And just then,
suddenly
there appears before you
that rabble with those words of evil prophecy
'Long live the end of the world!'
Not an inscription on a wall
but a trap
for extra-terrestrial beings.
Caught, you writhe
you die,
but the people read it impassively
and pass on.

That is the horror!

* * *

The walls and ceilings of reality,
the tunnels of our subconscious,
we have all suffered everything.
As the song has it:
the names of the idiots
and the wisdom of the vile
and the bequest of the killed
and the demagogy of the killers . . .

Every living being has sucked
the milk of fear
and of death.

But that slogan
'Long live the end of the world!'
was it conceived in a human brain
and painted
by a human hand?
No!
Here is no despair,
here is no black humour,
here is no touch of schizophrenia,
here is no obscurantism!

I'd say that this is the End . . .
But I don't wish for it!
'Long live the end . . .!'
Ecclesiastes and Nostradamus
did not express themselves thus.

But, of course, it is here and real . . .
And, of course,
we must be ever vigilant!
And, of course,
everyone, more than ever,
is responsible for the world!

*   *   *

My dear friend,
that night
in Paris,
in the cradle of pain,
strangled by lunar loneliness,
you opened
the cage of poetry,
you made
that old but faithful breeze
reach us
to warn us.

I'm grateful to you!
My dear friend,
I'll now go out and paint
my only answer everywhere:
'Long live
the world
without beginning and without end!'
I'll now go out and paint it on the walls . . .
But I think that's not enough,
my dear friend . . .
That's not enough!

(Note: On 12 September 1977 Levchev had received a letter from the French poet Pierre
Seghers who, deeply shocked, told him he had seen the slogan 'Long live the end of
the world' painted on a wall in the Paris Metro.)

ABANDONED CHURCHES

A heart without love is like
a church without God.
When the neighbours suspect that no one's there
they'll enter
and start pulling it apart –
a slab from the altar,
a piece of tiling,
an icon-lamp . . .
why, just for souvenirs!
And afterwards the real thieves will come.

A heart without love
experiences joy
even when torn apart.
But how terrible is a dying church!

The best thing then is to spread a rumour
that spectres are
haunting
the abandoned church,
stalking at night, knife in hand,
and in daytime swinging
from the chandeliers . . .

After that expect
heaven to send a flash of lightning,
so that your church burns down
immaculate.

A CASUAL SONG

Poet,
leave the poets now
and act as a pilot.

When the storm breaks,
when the heavens flare with hatred
and destruction sends out its cordial greetings,
and the round headlights
are like haloes without saints . . .

Poet,
then open the door of the cabin
and pass through,
smiling and content,
and pass through
like an off-hand song . . .

Poet . . .

And think then of the child
who,
almost unseen,
watches you
through the gap
between two back-rests,
who is holding on
with his hand to your smile . . .
You are now
the last religion,
poet!

But only
if you think of that child.

THE LAST CHILD

Here
is a child
on a pavement.
Here
is a child
with a big black stick.

Oh what a job he has to clean
his muddy shoes!

Yes,
he ran about with children and dogs
across the park,
across the grass,
across unexplored and nameless seas
and islands, across crunching and dirty snow.

Yes,
he fell like a kite
through a hundred invisible feats of heroism
and then rose up again.
He gave himself fully to the holiday air
and to himself . . .
Until
suddenly he saw
the trap of the great sorcerer.
Time!

The magic rays
were cutting across branches of silence,
the square little garden,
four streets
and pavements . . .

And the whole universe
was depopulated.

And there was no one left to ask:
'What's the time?'
The gluttonous souls
had all
left to perform sacred rituals.

All the children had grown up.
(What crazy time had elapsed since!)
And had grown wise.
(Not to say: grown old!)
And they were pure.
And they were sitting in their proper places
around the square-cut
table.

And then the Sunday fathers,
solemnly, as if in retribution,
spooned off their plates
the starry universe.
And blessed
the crumbs of life –
their children.
They blessed them . . .
Except one single father,
just imagine it,
all but one!

And so
the last child,
seized by panic and remorse,
tried desperately to remove
that treacherous mud.
He kicked at century-old trees.
He scraped the soles against the absurd notice:
'Don't pick the flowers –
they belong to you!'
And he felt like crying.

That's how it is,
of course –
after every feat
you find yourself soiled
and alone . . .

Aren't you,
my last reader,
aren't you perhaps, that last child?

TRUMPETER

I love the twilight.
Like those legendary trumpeters,
the evening
blood-stained
sounds
the eternal
retreat.
We don't hear . . .
But the flowers hear
and the worlds hear
up there
and rise . . .
That is the time to lie on the warm ground
and let the gentle grass caress you.
That is the time
for you
to drink the star's sap
in slow gulps.
And during those slow gulps you start to think:
Why should our eyes be so far-seeing?
Now
I don't hear the evening train
racing across the plain,
carrying my youth away . . .
Now
I don't feel the silver moth
entangled in my hair . . .
Yet I see Space!
For what?
It's not functional.
Why are we programmed to see
unimaginable spaces?
Why are we concerning ourselves
with the unattainable?

Stars!
Aren't you just nails in the universe?
What's fastened with you
I shan't ever know . . .

And yet before my eyes,
as though through triumphal arches,
your victorious troops are passing,
saluting Mother Infinity . . .

And so
in me
all weariness is dying.
And a new thirst being born.

ABSURD SELF-PORTRAIT OF BUREAUCRACY

But in effect
have I
not perhaps ceased
to exist
as a hope,
as a pain,
as a shaking, living person,
as a man?
Have I not been transformed
into some other substance?

Now I regard myself
reflected in the glass top
that protects the polish of the table –
a round table without knights.
Although this hour
is the reception hour,
all I receive is turbulent alarms . . .

Now I regard myself
reflected in the glass top
amidst little white clouds and pale ink.
I really am improbable!
My white
collar
gleams like the blade of a guillotine.
No!
What an absurd confession
to make to nothingness . . .
And my tie – a red one –
trickles down from my Adam's apple
and I can feel its stickiness
and warmth . . .
My suit:
official, black, indeed made of paper . . .
Surely, a pair of eyes can also be perceived?

Here, then,
a regular
passenger aircraft
soundlessly passes over the glass top
that protects the polish of the table.
And this time
it'll not crash into the ashtray,
nor into the alphabetical index,
nor into the vase
where
coloured pencils bloom.

It will pass across my forehead,
it'll become a paper aeroplane
and somehwere over there
it'll touch down.
The door will open
like a cursing mouth.
And then,
down an indigo gangway
the confidential notification will descend
that
perhaps
I have already ceased
to exist.

from
Afterlove
(1980)

LAST LOVE

In Homer's city –
down there in Homer's native city –
you're waiting for me,
my last love,
you're waiting for me . . .

Even when
wearied by snow-drifts
the stags come down to lick the asphalt . . .
you're waiting for me . . .

But when forebodings settle in the old
decaying garden-house,
and relatives
and silence,
when in the electric lamp
the filament starts singing . . .
and everybody says:
      It's burning out . . .
            It's burnt out . . .
                  Let's switch it off! . .
Will it then still be possible to wait?
That's why I'm off,
my last love,
to Homer's city –
down to his native city . . .

DÉNOUEMENT

You are undressing as if for the doctor.

The thought keeps splintering in my mind.
And suddenly
everything turns brittle.
The little vase becomes a test-tube,
The flower some strange bacillus.
And you are laughing at me:
– Come on, come on!
Ask me how I'm feeling.
And what my trouble is.
And where it hurts . . .
Ask what you will!
Only don't pretend . . .

And I bend down mechanically.
– Take a deep breath! –
                           I say.

                    *   *   *

And the air picks you up.
And you disappear.
You're no longer here.
The bed still holds your warmth –
the torn clothes of a fugitive.
But you've broken loose.
Forever.
Most likely you are now
descending
through memory.
You're crying.
And the zip of your skirt's torn.
And your voice is broken.

I hear:
Goodbye,
        darling,
                goodbye!
Goodbye, my love!
I wish you well –
and some of the pain.

ADVENTURE (A MADRIGAL)

Key and knife
hold my room.
What ordinary words they are –
key and knife!

Why do I need the key?
I hardly know.
I've no secrets,
I've no
bad
fears.

Besides,
behind lock and key
it only seems to me
that we should be together day and night.
(You know that love
is my delight.)

I sharpen my lead pencils
with a knife.
But I'm bound to tell you,
my dear comrades,
that the edge
of my genealogical strength
is not at all blunted.

Knife and key
don't
always meet
in one lair –
don't you agree?

But here
on returning
I find
a folded knife
on a key ring.

I realize that you've left, my love.
I even understand our separation now.
What made you think of leaving me this sign?
Easy to read
yet dangerous
as poppy-seed.

You're the key.
You patiently unlock
sweet truths and bitter truths.

I am the knife.
I'm the knife.
I cut these lines.

SHIPWRECK

Take care the wind doesn't wake you
when you're warm
and alone,
when you're dreaming a dream of mica
and of three necklaces of kisses . . .
Take care the wind doesn't wake you.
You'll rush out on deck,
bathed in cold
blue
shadows,
but suddenly you'll realize
that this is a most ordinary balcony.
You'll try to hoist
the fabulous sails
but you'll see above you
the pegged-out washing –
a toothed white jaw
ready to snap shut at any moment.
You'll rush to save
the thundering
sheet
that's breaking loose,
but from the other side
the wind
will tug at it with maddened nails.
And you'll rise on your toes.
Your breasts will be swaying
above the street
like lamps.
And the rail will cut
your belly
with a rusty knife.

I'm afraid.
The storm will carry you off.
Together with the sheet you'll fly away.
Just like a seagull with a fish it's caught
you'll rise up ever higher.

The chimney-stacks –
whales' heads –
strange fountains are erupting.
And furious shrieks will spatter you.
Jilted girl!
Jilted girl!
Jilted girl!
And in my madness
I know
that it'll seem to you
that the white sheet's
your diploma.

The girls from your student group,
the ugly ones
and the conscientious ones,
will pounce upon you with the pride of crows.
They'll pluck at you as an example:
    – What for?
    – Because the mistress is not immediately
returning to the Rhodope villages? . . .

And you'll cry.
And you'll never go back . . .

O my golden fish!
Mariner
from a ship of moonlit dreams!
I must be off now to a meeting.
You get your laundry done
and then
lie down in the cabin and go to sleep.
Draw all those rosy curtains.
Go dream your dreams of mica
and of three necklaces of kisses . . .
Our little boat will drift on
and the breeze
will be sighing
and like a glorious banner there'll be flying
my newly-washed white shirt.

ROMANTIC BALLAD

Maria –
a young widow,
widow of a surveyor –
with head erect and eyelids lowered
walked
through the garden.

And darkness fell and it was twice as black
as her black dress,
as her black stockings
and as the ribbon in her hair . . .

The poplars
like gossip-mongers
put their green heads together.
And a mute whisper drizzled on the park:
     – Her breasts are still firm . . .
     – Her eyes still imperious . . .
     – She's still a beauty . . .

Maria –
the young widow –
neither hears nor sees.
Some madness rises in her . . .
The birds are wakening with cheerful cheeps . . .
The dandelions are melting in the wind . . .

You really think this spring is useless?
You really think that love is dead?
You really think caresses are all buried?

– Good evening,
Maria . . .

Like the soft wings of a nocturnal moth
eye-lashes trembled with fright
above the fiery light
of eyes born to sight . . .

– Good evening,
Maria!
Don't be afraid of me.
I am
the carpenter's son,
the one who fell in the same battle
as your dead husband . . .

– Maria,
I'm an adult now . . .
Maybe because of that the war is over.
Tonight the soldiers fired
their last bullets
towards the sky . . .

– Maria,
you've been struck by the Moon.
The Moon has dropped among the ivy here.
And someone said:
' A perfect dancing floor!'
And someone said:
'I want to dance!'

– Maria –
I exclaimed –
I want to dance!
But I want to dance with you!

And spring came out trimphant.
From distant battlefields that no one knew
came all the trumpeters who had been killed.
And there they stood gigantic
and legs apart.
Their trumpets flashing bright amidst the black.
But they did not sound the attack . . .

What then rang out
was the most cheerful tune.
It scattered pollen on the cherry-trees.
And like a friend it said:
'You there, people,

time you lived
more wisely,
more beautifully,
more like humans!'

And so,
on that most perfect dancing floor,
those who were still alive
began to dance.
He danced, the son of the carpenter.
He danced with black Maria.
He danced with her
and kissed her.
All danced: the blizzard of the stars.
All danced: the elements of the sea.
All danced: the little birches which had snapped.
Even the road that had been mined . . .

The war was over.

Peace was beginning!

APPASIONATO

I love the night sky
because it alone is naked.
And this bright daylight prevents me
from seeking the nakedness of the universe.

Ah, that starry nakedness!

No, don't dress!
I want to find you.
To explore your substance
which so imperiously attracts me.

Love me!
Be my night!

TANGO

There is another earthly sphere
where everything is void of meaning.
Everything
except –
    that you've come
    that you're with me . . .
And that you're drinking a small chocolate brandy.

And the bad weather will be wonderful!

The rain will start on its career
as a pointillist.
So that you'll stay a long time,
                   a long time . . .

You are
the one
who makes things beautiful.
Even the broken umbrella stand.
Even the ladder on your knee,
stopped
with nail varnish.

And also:
you don't suspect
how beautiful you are . . .

There is another earthly sphere.

Why are you so jealous of me,
begrudging me the wind
and the evening's ebb
on the mountains?

CONTINUOUS POEM

Many evenings
before the birth
of our great intimacy
we used to meet
like glances:

– And what are you thinking of now?

We used to meet
like lips:

– And what are you thinking of now?

One evening
suddenly
we began
to reach each other's thoughts.
Simultaneously we smiled.
Quite simply: we set out.
I shielded you
with an embrace against the rain.

And shop-windows gilded us.
The pavements reflected us.
Drivers drove past us.
Women with children laughed at us.
And from afar came the fanfare salutes
of all our
past lovers . . .

We flew
and asked the shadows,
the winds,
the stars,
the drips from the gutters
and the telephone boxes:
– A spot for a pair of lovers!
In the library garden.
– A spot for a pair of lovers!

Under the smokestack of the Maritsa power plant.
– A spot for a pair of lovers!
On the breakwater at Burgas.

– A spot for a pair of lovers!
How small our country is!

– A spot for a pair of lovers!
How short our days appear!

How long shall I have to fly,
how long shall I be seeking
just a spot for a pair of lovers?

ULYSSES

I've been nowhere.
We're inseparable, we two
(like an actinia and a hermit crab.)
Nevertheless I keep returning
ceaselessly . . .
I don't know from where,
                              but I'm returning.

To you,
improbably, I keep returning.
Unrecognizable from love and wounds.
I'm returning as from an old legend . .

Why should I have this feeling all the time?

Yet you stand all alone on that breakwater,
where the surf of my thoughts is splintering.
Under the radar aerials on airfields,
where all my dreams touch down.
And on station platforms . . .

You call from far away:
                              I love you!
                              Welcome back!
                              I love you!

Thank you,
            dearest,
                        for the fact

that every moment without you is an Odyssey.
Thank you, dear, for waiting here for me.
And for this meeting . . .

Again
you embrace me.
I've returned.
And every single cell of yours
tells me how it's waited,
how it's burned
like some minute and lonely lighthouse . . .

And I'm weary of adventures.
And I'm happy to be close to you.

CAPRICE NO. 6

It's true that I am overburdened.
It's true that I carry a cargo of memories.
It's true that some are forbidden and dangerous . . .

I'm sailing with a list like some doomed ship.
– We'll drown! –
the captain shouts from within.
– Maybe –

     I say –

                  but we've nothing to jettison.

– The first big wave will send us down
to dine with the girls from Atlantis!
– So what, so what . . .
I'll try not to worry overmuch . . .

Don't I seem content?

I cross the 'Sound of Sweet Fatigue'.
I heave to in the 'Bay of Whispers'.
Your hand burns in my hand
like a shielded torch.

Like long ago
when I was invisible
the garden swings are rocking on their own,
you hear just their metallic exclamations
or the grating of armour
from some saga
or from some sombre ballad . . .

There my youth calls out:
Love,
how much you have given me!
Love,
how much you have taken from me!

But today I don't need your words!
I only need your voice.
I throw myself into it.
I hide my head as in my mother's lap.
I wriggle happily.
I'm sinking,
ever deeper,
ever deeper.
To where
girls from Atlantis
bring me amphoras of fragrant madness.

WE STOPPED

We stopped.
Right under the notice
'No stopping'.
And you said to me then:
– This is my favourite spot . . .

A bridge.
Of rails and planks.
That rusty rainbow.
And the notice
'No stopping'.

No river flows beneath the bridge.
Only a stream of railway lines.
And signals
waving their arms.
And thunderous roar of midnight manoeuvres.

And when
under our feet
some locomotive passed
the clouds of steam enveloped us.
And totally invisible
and totally alone
we kissed.

There must be millions of wagons
with cargoes of our kisses
dispatched to all
corners of the earth.
We moved on
when I said to you:
– This is my favourite spot . . .

A bridge.
Magnificent.
And unforgettable.
Between childhood and manhood.
And a notice:
'No stopping'.

CAPRICE NO. 11

The Sacred Volcano –
that woodcut,
carved with a few scratches
by Hokusai,
shines in my mind
more powerfully than reality
and far more credibly than it is in nature.

For the real mountain,
the real Fujiyama –
it's
so improbable
I could accept it only
as a dream,
as a sigh,
as an interjection . . .
Ah . . .

Its foot is lost
in a mist of tenderness.
Only its snow-capped crown
gleams in the sky like a phantom,
like a balcony,
but
one that projects from the void of the universe,
from the castle of the unknown.

I wouldn't believe my eyes
if I didn't know
that such a heavenly
balcony
improbably
also floats inside me.
Once in a few million
years
you step out on it,
my love.
You step out to see if there are any stars.

But instead you discover
a murderous
sombre
man.

I love you!
This whisper at the very end,
this final word,
has thrown out all its meaning
so it can carry
all its feeling . . .
I love you!

No.
That's no word.
That surely is the ultimate particle
that's left of me.
The ultimate real something
that I have . . .
Take it!

from
Incantations
(1981)

MADRIGAL

I know you well.
You're not a cloud
from which a thunderbolt might crash
or blessed rain
might fall.
That's the privilege of lowering,
menacing, wild and murky skies.
But you're a cloudlet in a snow-white jacket,
the darling of the sun itself,
and you will proudly gleam on high
till the next wind.

BELATED WORDS

White wine with white-heart cherries.
Ridiculous recollection from my youth.
Oh what a sinner I was.
What a sinner!
The happiest
in the world.
A steep little street.
A lilac shrine.
And a kiss, awkward and boyish.
And still the wind is looking for
my student cap.
Snow follows me,
all fragrant in my heart –
measureless silence and
some measured verse.

This is the smell
only of trees
doomed to be felled.

EPITAPH

I was strong once.
I could have been
a stonemason
or else a righteous man.
And so I just survived my wounds
and leave now as an optimist.
All-Highest,
All-Gracious,
our dear Father,
forgive my mortal sins, and worse!
If nothing else,
at least I had the guts
to claim there's sense in writing verse.

HUNGER

The children in Kampuchea
are playing with skulls.
Eyes and sockets silent
and relentless
are fixed on you.
First greeting
              and final reproach
to this compassionless world.
Children are playing with skulls.
By now they're only a picture in a journal.
Under the headling 'Hunger!'
              Hunger!
              Hunger!
How does the word ring
in your ears, well-fed European?
You
who keep a fresh-fruit diet
(but then the heart grows fat)
don't you feel any disquiet?
Any remorse?

You feel your own repletion like a pain.
You'll die of a quite different
more terrible hunger,
a kind so far not diagnosed.
When you've fed historically
you'll suddenly understand
that your mission is not to be a consumer.

Hunger has killed
your sense of hunger, made you numb.

Maybe this is
the shape of things to come?

          *   *   *

You
who are turning back from the abyss
of repletion,
why are you silent?
Why don't you warn us?
Why don't you scream?

Ernest,
stop cleaning your rifle
while it's loaded!
Don't annoy me
while the insane flamenco
of Lucerno Tena is aflame.
Or . . is this already
impossible?
You've long ceased to be living people.
You're just spectres, dressed
in costumes of dignity
behind masks of humour . . .

*   *   *

And I begin my secret fantasies:
A man without food –
After a month
or a little more
will die.
And without water –
after four or five days and nights at most.
And without oxygen
after three minutes he'll meet
his Maker.

And without love?
Without that shining faith?
After how long, mankind, does your spirit
die?

Science
isn't concerned
with such untechnological domains.
So that
perhaps
now only poetry remains?

*   *   *

The children in Kampuchea
are playing with skulls.
There
among them
you'll find Prince Hamlet.
And then maybe
right at the end
we too will play with some vague object
in our hands.

REQUIEM

Summer's gone.
      The birds have gone.
You've gone . . .
Outside the Vagankovka cemetery
the wind's opening and shutting
the telephone boxes.
The maple foliage is on fire
and the smoke
reaches out
with long and thin and dusky nails
for the sky's face.
As if somebody there were suffocating
and struggling to snatch something
and get away.
Yes,
things really are frightfully tight
in there
among the lanes.
The little graves are getting even smaller.
The crosses, wrought-iron and stone, are jostling like
old women in a queue for eternity.
I didn't spot a single well-known star.
Apart from you,
Volodya,
my brother –
your Highness Vysotskiy.

You're lying
there
on the very edge
and by the gate,
where strangers feed the pigeons.
You're lying
alone,
a stranger, pigeon and food for pigeons . . .
But haven't they appointed you janitor?

If so,
then
warn them, I beg you,
shout, sing, whisper . . .
(You can do anything.)
Let everyone know
that it's no longer possible to die.
There's no room left
either on earth
or in heaven!
There's no room left
beyond the rotten and inexplicable fence!
A short while more
and death will spill over it
like boiling milk
forgotten on a stove.
And it will run out.
And will mingle with life.
And everything will become explicable.
And that will be the end of the world . . .
Don't let any more in,
Volodya!
Tell them they've got to live!
Tell them they've got to resurrect!
Tell them you've saved
a tiny spot
only for me.
Because we've something important to say to each other.
Because I've got to make
one
totally inexplicable poem.
In it we shall appear
and in it we shall vanish
as soon
as
night
falls.

Note: The Vagankovka cemetery is in Leningrad

THE LAW

(for Damyan P. Damyanov)

Those kings of the snobbish cafés
will never forgive us
that we were Komsomol poets
and glorified
the smoke of Kremikovtsi.
And at the same time listened to Gershwin
or translated Eliot.
But we remained
true unto death
to our manly nation.
And now, with hearts battered
by responsibilities
and love,
we continue to examine
youth's
savage
law.

The law's short.
It commands:
You shall serve human beauty!
And don't exchange your conscience for any
fame or glory!

Note: Kremikovtsi is the name of a steelworks outside Sofia.

PRAYER FOR THE VARNA PAINTERS

The sailors say
there are two seas:
the sea on this side
and the sea beyond the horizon.

On this side is our familiar sea
stretching away from the shore –
a sea for joy
and for summer.

And beyond . . .

There gleams the abyss, with dangers to the spirit.
There, like an accursed frigate
creative torment roams . . .
There every wave is the ninth,
there ozone blows and hatred . . .

Boys beyond the horizon,
may albatrosses guard you!

DREAMS

Dreams come flying like birds.
Migratory signs.
Heavenly letters.
Aspirations.
And they circle
above me,
they circle
after their perilous flight
across wastes of lost consciousness.

Dreams come flying like birds.
Looking for a nest.
But there –
my night thoughts twist,
their lunar eyes
and teeth are flashing,
and you can hear the throbbing of
their angry hearts.

Dreams fly away like birds . . .

Tonight another will be dreaming you.

AUTUMNAL REVELATION

for Tamara

In spite of everything
autumn takes me by surprise.
And I
once again stand before it like a child.
I feel nostalgic about departing birds.
I converse with the spectral falling of the leaves.
Beaten gold,
filtering between tree-trunks,
rustles under my feet.
And I reflect
that these are not just leaves
but that the sun has died . . .

And
honestly
I don't know what death is.

ENIGMA

Are you still waiting for me there –
on the bridge without a road
and under
a star without a name?

I don't know.
Because I said sometimes:
– Let me go, my love!
And I entered into you
as into a dangerous sanctuary.
Through your enchanted eyes,
through the flash of your tear
I entered into you,
my love . . .
And today I understand that I flare
in the light of mirrors.
Your soul reflects me,
my love.
From you my own eyes
look on me.

In your every fibre I view myself –
a giant here
and there a ridiculous little boy.
I lose myself
and hit myself
and there's no way out
for my reflection with the bleeding lips.
And I shan't ever come out
from you,
my love.

And you're waiting for me still
on the bridge without a road
and under
a star without a name.